s/13

LANCÔME

First published in the United States of America in 1999
by UNIVERSE PUBLISHING
A Division of Rizzoli International Publications, Inc.
300 Park Avenue South
New York, NY 10010

and

THE VENDOME PRESS

Translated from the French by Richard Maxwell

Front cover photograph: Bottle created by Jean Sala, limited edition, 1944.
© Photo: Laziz Hamani/Éditions Assouline.

Back cover photograph: *Marrakech*, bottle designed by Marc Lalique.
© Photo: Laziz Hamani/Éditions Assouline

ISBN: 0-7893-0327-2

Printed in Italy

Library of Congress Catalog Card Number: 98-61801

99 00 01 02 / 10 9 8 7 6 5 4 3 2 1

UNIVERSE OF BEAUTY

LANCÔME

By Jacqueline Demornex

UNIVERSE / VENDOME

When Armand Petitjean founded Lancôme in 1935 he was already fifty years old, with several careers, several countries, and several lives behind him. These previous lives were to influence the development of the brand's identity, and he was never to forget South America, where he had long worked as an importer of manufactured goods from Europe; nor would he forget his successful period with the French Foreign Office. And then there was his collaboration with François Coty, who had initiated him to the perfumer's subtle art, and from whom he had just parted, to create his own brand.

Coty was renowned as the father of modern perfumery, and had created rare and exclusive fragrances, but in Petitjean's eyes he had committed the ultimate crime: in search of volume, he had gone down-market. Armand Petitjean was going to take up the challenge; his was to be a prestige brand, or nothing.

And he was not alone. A group of colleagues was ready to undertake the adventure with him. Among them were the d'Ornano brothers, the chemist Pierre Velon, and Georges Delhomme, Coty's former design director. All of them had admired their leader, all had felt deceived by the new turn of events.

While they were creating their first products, Armand Petitjean was also searching for a name for their new business. At one point he considered using the name of the village where he was born, Saint-Loup, but it did not sound feminine. He dreamed of a name that would have a truly French sound, that would echo famous historical names like Brantôme, Vendôme.... Guillaume d'Ornano suggested the name of a château in the Indre department, named Lancosme. All they had to do was to change the silent "s" for a circumflex , and the result was perfect—a French name that everyone could pronounce, written with the specifically French circumflex. Lancôme, symbol of France.

Armand Petitjean was short, with a meticulously kept moustache and pointed beard, always impeccably dressed with pastel shirts, white collar and cuffs. He was extremely courteous, always taking his hat off to even his humblest employee, but his eyes—an innocent sky-blue when he wanted to charm someone—could change in a second to a steely gaze. He was, it seemed, always on his guard, always totally self-controlled, in the service of the task he had set himself.

"Why did I create Lancôme?" he said one day, "Because I had seen that two American brands had taken control of the beauty industry. A French brand should be up alongside them."

Petitjean orchestrated Lancôme's first appearance with great skill. In 1935, he launched five new fragrances simultaneously, presenting them to the world at the June opening of the Universal Exhibition in Brussels. For the period, these were surprising perfumes, surprisingly packaged, with a richly baroque character at odds with the fashion for minimalism. *Tropiques, Conquête, Kypre, Tendres Nuits,* and *Bocages,* as well as their bottles ornamented with gold, orchids, green forests, or moldings of cargo ropes, were a snub to the ascetically geometric Art Deco of the moment. As their creator, Georges Delhomme, was to say later, "During the thirties, less of anything

5

was more chic. In your apartment, nothing on the walls. If you had a new painting, you showed it to visitors, then put it away. Perfume bottles were square or rectangular, flat. We wanted to do the opposite."

This quintuple launch had been carefully calculated. For Armand Petitjean, a perfumer didn't exist unless he had international status. He had to offer fragrances to suit every taste, for all women, on all five continents. In fact, Petitjean succeeded in capturing a world of multiple cultures in each fragrance. Here's how he described his perfumes some years later to a class of *techniciennes* at the Ecole Lancôme:

"...*Tropiques* is like honey. With its heavy coating of spices and aromatics it frightens off most of the English and the northerners, although it may appeal profoundly to women of society and artists. *Conquête*, a concentrated fragrance of roses on a chypre base, will please any woman who likes to be noticed when she enters the theatre or a restaurant. The freshness and relaxed style of *Bocages* is perfect for younger women and will seduce Swedes, Norwegians, Belgians, Germans, and the women of northern France. *Kypre* should be treated like a Burgundy; it needs to age in the bottle, like the wine. In our climate, it is more of a perfume for winter and for festivities, but in the East and in South America, it appeals in all seasons...."

the man who created these five fragrances was, *bien sûr*, very attracted to women. And whether they were from the north or the south, society ladies or artists, he dreamed of them as, above all, elegant. One of the earliest advertisements for Lancôme shows us two women, a brunette and a blonde, wearing sumptuous negligees and seated by a long oval dressing mirror. The silky garments flow over their bodies, illustrating without revealing; their hair is permed, their eyebrows plucked; and the blonde is holding the special Lancôme perfume bottle, its stopper encrusted with glass jasmine flowers. It is the quintessence of thirties' elegance and of Petitjean's idea of beauty, which he saw as inextricably associated with elegance. And isn't elegance what France does best?

The result of the launch was excellent for the image of Lancôme; the five fragrances won a double medal at the Brussels exhibition. But sales figures were less brilliant—perfumeries didn't know what to make of this new-born brand and didn't support the product. Petitjean's bold gesture, however, clearly revealed the heights of his ambition.

The following year, he nevertheless had his feet firmly on the ground and let fall this historic description: "Perfume is prestige, the flower in your buttonhole. But beauty products are our daily bread."

Because he wanted to reinvent the concept of beauty he turned to science, with the aid of Dr. Medynski, a professor at the veterinary research establishment in Maisons-Alfort, just outside Paris. He had recently discovered how to stabilize horse serum, an essential step in creating more effective skin-care products. Together, Medynski and the industrial chemist Pierre Velon perfected a nutrient cream which contained not only natural serum but also active ingredients based on proteins and vitamins. This innovation was called *Nutrix*. "*La Nutrix*," as it was known, was described as "a regenerating night cream," and quickly became a panacea, used for sunburn, stings from plants and insects, chilblains, frostbite, and razor burn. The British minister of defense even recommended it in the fifties as the only known remedy for radiation burns in case of nuclear war....

The sales promise, too, was astonishingly in advance of its time: "*Nutrix* guards against skin deficiencies by encouraging the skin's self-defense mechanisms." It is an approach which foreshadows the biomimetic research that is one of the major activities of Lancôme today. In passing, it is noteworthy that *Nutrix* has become a skin-care product fetish and still has many supporters.

In 1938, Lancôme makeup, which had been in existence since 1935, took its turn center stage, when Armand Petitjean created another counter-current product. At that time, the fashion was for indelible lipsticks that lasted because they dyed the lip tissues. Unfortunately, they also dried out the lips. Petitjean created *Rose de France*, a pale pink lipstick with a soft texture that would give the customer "lips...soft and gleaming like a baby's." It was a sensual product, with a rose fragrance, and, supported by the *Conquête* line of face powders (in eighteen shades, from golden brown to palest ivory), it was to be a best seller until the fifties.

t he brand had rapidly established itself with three branches of cosmetic activity, each with its own emblem: a rose for perfumery, a cherub for makeup, and a lotus flower for skin-care products. In 1939, Lancôme was only four years old but had already established its international ambitions by opening up markets in all the corners of the world. Orders were coming in from Oslo, Bogotá, Algiers, Shanghai.... And it was at this point that World War II broke out.

The War in 1914 had changed Armand Petitjean's destiny in South America, from importer to international man of affairs and spokesman for the French government. And in France, his new-born business had been a cosmetics producer like its competitors until World War II. But the shortage of materials meant halting production of fragrances, makeup, and skin-care products. The product catalog shrank. As happens with brilliant minds, this setback inspired a brilliant response. If production is restricted, we must use what we've got.

Why not concentrate on training our people to the highest levels?

It was in this spirit that he created the Ecole Lancôme, whose first classes were held in Paris on February 9, 1942, at the height of the war. Petitjean, who after the first great European conflagration had refused offers of posts as Ambassador and as Minister of Propaganda in Clemenceau's government, was now preparing to train a battalion of women to be ambassadors for Lancôme. It was his philosophy that these ambassadors would be the most elegant, most efficient communicators of the Lancôme message. They could accomplish more than advertising. They were to promote the values of the brand and of French culture by demonstration and through what he called "propaganda." He was convinced that direct word-of-mouth communication was the surest way to build a reputation. And, who better than women, trained and knowledgeable women, to talk to other women about beauty? Lancôme, already the first cosmetics company to be conceived as a vehicle for cultural values, thus evolved a purpose-designed training center, where technical representatives were trained to promote Lancôme—and thus, France—far and wide.

hand-picked students—never more than twenty—received a thorough scientific and artistic training at the Ecole Lancôme. They studied anatomy and physiology, the technology of skin-care products and the techniques of selling (hence the name "*techniciennes*"). They had courses in drawing and modelling, in makeup—Charles Dullin, one of France's leading theatrical personalities came to teach stage makeup—and of course, massage and auto-massage. Massage was at that period very much in vogue, with books on beauty devoting whole chapters to the subject.

"The true preventative against the stigmata of premature aging is facial massage," reads Marie Marelli's *Les soins de beauté scientifiques*, a very popular book published in 1936. One of the great names in this field was Professor Leroy, recognized as a master of massage at the Imperial Court of Japan, and it was one of Leroy's pupils with an international reputation, Dr. Durey, who became the Ecole Lancôme's massage teacher. Surprisingly, he taught a special system of facial massage without cream or oil, *le massage à sec*, developed especially for Lancôme, because it enabled a more precise massage of the delicate facial tissues.

But Dr. Durey's massage went further than the simple physical treatment. He insisted that the body and mind had to be treated together. "You can only give an effective treatment if you are sympathetic," he wrote, "The beauty adviser who feels, 'How pleased I shall be to see this woman become more beautiful,' already has hands that have unconsciously become more tender, more adaptable and benefic; waves of energy flow through her in an instinctively beneficent rhythm. As the treatment begins, movement by movement a harmony is created between the two people. The aura of the beauty adviser is activated. The patient relaxes, even sleeps." This is a massage, and a message, that the Institut Lancôme could still be proud of today.

The perfumery course was given by Armand Petitjean himself. There exists a copy of his course notes, typed on onion-skin paper. And as he left no interviews, it is the only record of the way he spoke. Here we find the trace of Coty, the great Coty at the height of his powers and fame: "Coty was a builder. In front of his *château* at Montbazon, he had a terrace built that created the same impression as his fragrances: clear, solid, magnificent. In his view, a drawing room could not be other than circular or oval. Galleries had to be broad. His fragrances were conceived along just these lines."

Petitjean regretted the passing of the fashion for clear fragrances—those from a single flower. This was mostly because of the influence of the couturiers, who introduced far more complicated perfumes and made women accustomed to violent and powerful scents.

In expressing his strong opinions, Petitjean was a master of the sound bite, once saying, *"l'art du parfumeur est de fixer l'aérien"*—"the perfumer's art is 'to give to airy nothing a local place of habitation and a name'" (borrowing an equivalent turn of phrase from Shakespeare). Explaining that certain perfumes change in contact with different types of skin, especially if the woman is taking medicines, he said, "Arthritis and red hair are the death of jasmine." His character comes through clearly from these notes: *"Conquête* was a demonstration of willpower. Mine. *Conquête* was a symbol. It was necessary to conquer the world to make the reputation of Lancôme."

a fter the war, Petitjean was indeed able to survey a number of conquests. While his perfumes hadn't in fact conquered the world—events were, to say the least, unfavorable—he had been able to conquer a wide feminine market: the skin-care market. Because of his rigorous "no substitutes" policy of quality at all costs, he had created *"Nutrix* hunger" and an effective word-of-mouth support for Lancôme skin-care products.

But Armand Petitjean the perfumer was fretting with impatience, and in 1947, he launched *Marrakech*. The bottle, an amphora flanked by palmettos in solid glass, had been designed by Marc Lalique, but the technical problems were too great. He passed the project to Georges Delhomme, whose hands-on knowledge of glass and glassmakers was unequalled ("You have to get your face burned over the furnace to understand"). He got it right the first time. This beautiful bottle and its magnificent presentation case, which today earns record prices at auction, were the forerunners of the brilliant launches to follow.

In 1950, perhaps the apogee of Petitjean's administration, Lancôme launched *Magie*. Petitjean had dreamed of this perfume for years. He had conceived of the fragrance, based on aromatic woods and splashes of jasmine, and had made over a thousand tests with George Leplieux, the Lancôme "nose." His conception for the bottle was a crystal torsade, which was brought to life by Georges Delhomme. It was perhaps one of the most spectacular creations of the fifties.

Two years later *Trésor*, the first *Trésor*, was born. This was a refined oriental perfume, presented in a sumptuous crystalline container cut like a diamond. To celebrate the launch, Petitjean held a grand *fête* at the Palais de Chaillot, in Paris, at which guests could watch *Trésor* dance with *Magie* in a ballet by Serge Lifar, with music by Henri Sauguet. Some very pretty pages of advertising from the period still exist in the Lancôme museum. One shows the bottles set against a starry night sky; the other, also against a background of stars, has two fairy-tale characters, the Eastern Prince *Trésor* tenderly holding the hand of the fairy *Magie*. The two were inseparable, at least in the world of advertising.

during these early years of the fifties, Armand Petitjean was a contented man. His family life made him very happy. He lived at *Les Vallières*, a villa surrounded by extensive grounds, dominated by one of the most majestic Gingko trees in France, with a rose garden that was celebrated for its perfection. His wife Nelly was a passionate orchid grower and a talented flower arranger, whose bouquets and table decorations were a delight. Sunday lunch was a real family institution, with fifteen people (including seven children) and at least two or three guests whom Petitjean wished to honor. These included writers such as Jean Giraudoux, eminent medical specialists, and also potential Lancômian high-fliers being given a look-over by the *patron* himself.

On weekdays, he was a regular restaurant-goer. Lunch at Maxim's or Lucas Carton, meals at Lapérouse with the *techniciennes*, and every New Year a grand dinner at the Plaza Athénée for all the executives. Women got out their long dresses; men rented dinner jackets; and after speeches and a meal of splendor and elegance, all worked out to the last detail, there was music and dancing until dawn. Petitjean loved to dance, especially the waltz and the tango.

For the great charity balls and other high society events which were held at this period, he provided gifts of his fragrances in specially created, limited-edition bottles. Some, such as *Bouquet de Violettes* or *Les Danseurs*, have become extremely rare.

Petitjean the businessman was as happily situated as Petitjean the family man. His succession was assured—not by his son, Armand-Marcel, who had always said he would never work for his father, "that magnificent tyrant," but by his grandson, Jean-Claude, who accompanied his grandfather everywhere, studied perfumery at the plant, learned ten languages, was an accomplished sportsman and athlete, and was being brought up as the future Lancôme Superman.

The brand image was equally satisfying: *Magie* and *Trésor* had raised Petitjean to the status of a great name in perfumery, and women fought for his lipsticks in their finely wrought golden cases, manufactured at his jewelry plant near Annecy.

And his *techniciennes*, his international ambassadors, were spreading the good word all over the world. In Moscow, Nina Gaucher, of Russian descent, charmed President Khruschev and won an order of grandiose dimensions. Cécile Cristofini was sent to Central America, where Armand Petitjean asked her to persuade the local agent to pay her expenses—her ticket alone had already cost him a small fortune. The local agent agreed—and in the next few months Cécile gave personal makeup instruction to more than a thousand women.... In New York, Simone de Reyssi, the little Parisienne, had an outrageous impact. She lunched every day at *La Potinière*, surrounded by buyers and journalists. One of them wrote, "Before you've finished your coffee, Simone's magic has worked its spell and you're convinced that *Magie* is the only fragrance in the world...." Wherever they went, Lancôme's ambassadresses were received like stars. In Africa, heads of state and governors welcomed them to their palaces. In Australia, there were television interviews; everywhere they went there was a half-page in the biggest daily paper.... But to win this influence, these women had had to learn it all, not just the physiology and drawing and languages, but how to do everything, from skin-care treatments and makeup to assisting a regional representative with local customs, obtaining import licenses, packaging shipments, replacing a representative at a moment's notice, developing new markets, and, of course, sending a daily report to "Monsieur P."

Monsieur P. had succeeded in his effort to expand his markets. Restrained during the war and the years immediately after it, exports were now booming. In 1955, Lancôme products were on sale in 98 countries through 33 general agents, of which nine were direct subsidiaries. Lancôme's representatives were tireless—some of them even went literally around the world twice a year. Naturally, some countries were less welcoming—China, for example. But Armand Petitjean made no secret of his ambition—"I dream of one day selling a lipstick to every woman in China." He had built his empire; he was its uncontested sovereign and deserved his nickname—Armand the Magnificent.

but states of grace do not last long, and suddenly it seemed that fortune, so long at his elbow, had deserted him. In 1955, Petitjean's wife died. He was devastated by her loss and seemed to lose something of himself. The following year, his adored grandson, Jean-Claude, decided that he was going to go his own way and that he would not join Lancôme. Suddenly, Petitjean felt that he had built his castle on sand.... His control of the company— especially his emphasis on performance and quality in new product development—led to complications.

For the next surge of activity, he had put all his hopes in the newly developed *Océane* line. It was in advance of its time—this was nothing new for Lancôme—but it was too complicated. Based on the use of seawater and marine extracts, there were too many products with complicated classical names—*Aphrodite, Triton, Nérée, Neptune,* and so on. Add the problems of a new system of classifying skin types that had five different categories, and it was clear that both representatives and distributors were going to lose their way, not to mention the consumers.

As he faced personal difficulties, he held on tighter to old certainties. At this period, he turned down an idea that was to revolutionize makeup sales, because it upset his notions of elegance. The new invention he was offered was the disposable lipstick case. "No woman worthy of the name would ever put such a horror in her handbag!" he exclaimed. He could not imagine for one second that an elegant woman, who chose her accessories with care, could ever prefer a shoddy plastic tube to his jewel-like gold-plated cases with their finely sculpted designs.... The competition seized on the novelty, and Lancôme's magnificent lipstick holders—*Shaker, Clé de Coquette,* and similar masterpieces of cosmetic jewelery—went into a free fall.

a nd it was just at this uncertain point in his fortunes that work had been started on Petitjean's show-piece production plant at Chevilly-Larue, located on the National 7 highway near Orly, the main airport for Paris. The ground had been purchased back in 1950 and marked off all around by an imposing iron grill. Within this fence was a superb estate consisting, for the moment, of shrubs and rose bushes. Early in 1957, the first stone was laid. The walls were to be of creamy Poitou stone, which keeps its color over time, and the roofing of Fumay slate, which at sunset takes on a purple tinge. Petitjean was driven to the site every day and told himself and many others that visitors leaving France from Orly would carry away, as their last memory, the sight of Lancôme's name spelled out in gold letters along the road to the airport. He had not foreseen the A6 motorway to Orly nor the new international airport that would be built at Roissy, north of Paris.

In 1961, the company's financial situation became critical. Believing that he had no successor, Petitjean had poured his own fortune and that of Lancôme into the construction of the new plant at Chevilly, just at a time when the cosmetics market was changing. The debts mounted up until the director of the company's bank contacted Armand-Marcel Petitjean to tell him, "We no longer have confidence in your father. Lancôme is a family concern. If the family doesn't shoulder its responsibilities, we shall cut off all credit. You have 48 hours to make your decisions."

It would shake anyone. But although Armand-Marcel had no business experience—he is a writer—he squared up to the task and took over from his father as provisional managing director, just at the moment the new plant was completed. So it was under his guidance that the move from Courbevoie to Chevilly was carried out, and on June 20, 1962, this aesthetically superb but functionally flawed *"Versailles de la Parfumerie"* was inaugurated with great pomp and circumstance. The *Garde Nationale* formed an honor guard for personalities from politics and society. The weather was superb. The official photograph is a curious and moving document. It shows Armand and Armand-Marcel. Armand-Marcel is certainly looking at his father—watchfully? anxiously? But what is Armand the Magnificent really looking at with that quizzical expression? He seems to be gazing past his son at the splendid buildings, his lifetime's achievement, which he is now powerless to touch.

Armand-Marcel was to spend three years at the helm of Lancôme. Three years during which he had to try and adapt the brand to the new realities of the market. The Lancôme team closed ranks and backed him loyally. Agents around the world responded nobly, often ordering products for a year or two ahead. Naturally, once they were overstocked, they would not be able to reorder easily, but Lancôme desperately needed the money, both to pay off the mountainous debts and to maintain a viable level of activity in product creation and sales development.

Slowly at first, but then with increasing weight, the evidence piled up. Not only the banks realized the gravity of the situation, but the whole family was finally forced to see that the time had come to sell the business.

Suitors were not lacking. Rumor spoke of Revlon, Yardley, Payot. They all had a defect in common—they were not French.

When François Dalle contacted the Petitjean family, his offer was built around the new financial vigor he could provide, using L'Oréal's wide market penetration and very deep pockets to rejuvenate and give fresh impetus to the rich Lancôme heritage. Negotiations were opened and finally concluded under conditions that satisfied both sides. Armand Petitjean died on September 29, 1970. He was 84 years old and had lived enough for three lifetimes. He had started modestly, had made and lost fortunes, had been an influential figure in the fierce excitements of the twentieth century, consorting with presidents and princes and the leading intellects and creative spirits of the day. It would please him to know that Lancôme today sells thousands of lipsticks to the women of China, even if they are in disposable containers.

1ancôme today is the leading French brand in selective perfumery, present in 163 countries. The infusion of energy and marketing know-how provided by L'Oréal has provided the strength needed to ensure Lancôme's survival without compromising the values that make up "the Lancôme spirit."

French cultural values and the French perception of elegance and beauty as a whole are still at the heart of the brand's identity. The spirit of conquest and adventure is dynamically successful on a world-wide scale. The spirit of innovation has been amplified and perfected thanks to the extraordinary capacities of the L'Oréal laboratories, which reserve their most striking discoveries for Lancôme, the group's flagship brand. Almost every recent advance in skin-care products has been the fruit of this integrated effort. The spirit of creativity and joy is fully expressed through Lancôme's renowned makeup branch, with explosions of energy and imagination in every new collection. And the spirit of Petitjean's original concept, of Lancôme as a great perfume house, is demonstrated in all its subtle glory with successes such as *Trésor*, *Poême*, and *Ô oui!*

Today, Juliette Binoche, Inès Sastre, Cristiana Reali, and Marie Gillain, like Isabella Rossellini before them, offer their multiple appeal to every woman in every country in the world. And in every major airport you will find the smile of one or the other of them and the phrase, "France has a word for beauty: Lancôme."

Armand Petitjean himself could well have chosen such a description of his dream, a dream which has today become a planet-wide reality. As the new millennium approaches, Lancôme has become what he dreamed it should be....

MARRAKECH

Atmosphère secrète des demeures et des tentes seigneuriales,
souffles parfumés des orangeraies et des jardins mauresques,
violents relents des caravanes arrêtées.

PRÉSENTATION ORIGINALE

Flacon de Lalique enserrant dans un encadrement en verre clair massif
orné de palmettes et posé sur pied,
l'amphore aux lignes dépouillées et à long col
où brille le parfum de nuance topaze.

Coffret vertical à 8 pans inégaux, couronné d'un toit à créneaux
et décorés de panneaux verts et rouges rehaussés d'or,
s'ouvrant comme un paravent pour présenter le flacon
sur un socle vermillon et blanc
devant un fond de paysage évoquant l'oasis au bord du désert.

2 TAILLES

30 gr. ou 1 oz. Réf. 5501
60 gr. ou 2 oz. Réf. 5503

Lascif, capiteux et opiniâtre, à note sauvage et pourtant précieux,
parfum d'aventure et de voyage.

LANCÔME

PARFUMS

SOINS DE LA PEAU   MAQUILLAGE

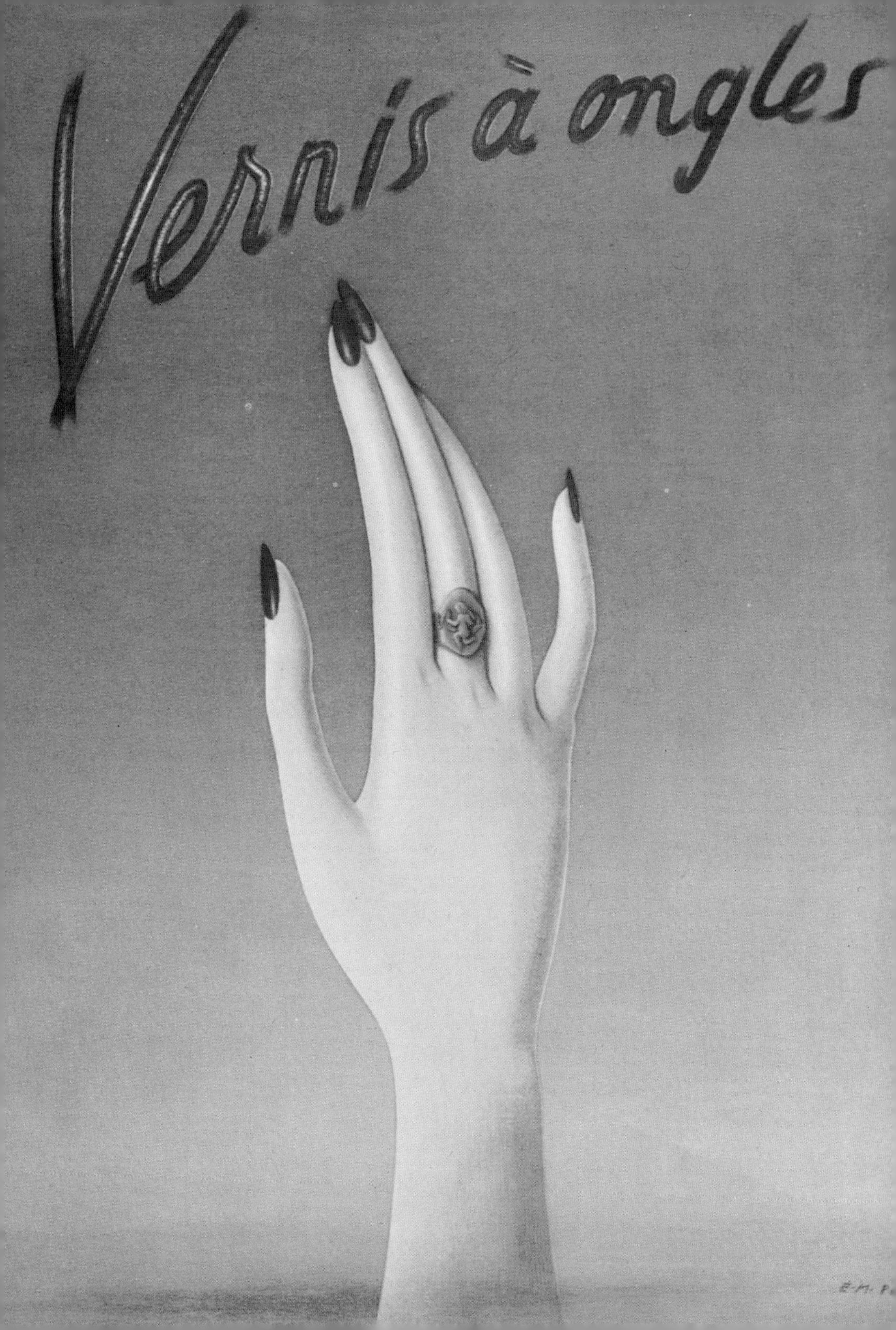
Vernis à ongles

13924 Prioux
R.R. 35353
Vélin alfa teinté crème
65 × 100 de 28 kl.

13925 Prioux
R.R. 35313
Vélin alfa teinté crème
65 × 100 de 28 kl.

LANCÔME FRANCE
GARANTIT LA HAUTE QUALITÉ DU PRODUIT ET LA PERFECTION DE LA FABRICATION
N° 1 VERMEIL

LANCÔME FRANCE
GARANTIT LA HAUTE QUALITÉ DU PRODUIT ET LA PERFECTION DE LA FABRICATION
N° 5 FEU

LANCÔME FRANCE
GARANTIT LA HAUTE QUALITÉ DU PRODUIT ET LA PERFECTION DE LA FABRICATION
N° 9 ORANGÉ

LANCÔME FRANCE
GARANTIT LA HAUTE QUALITÉ DU PRODUIT ET LA PERFECTION DE LA FABRICATION
N° 10 INCARNAT

LANCÔME FRANCE
GARANTIT LA HAUTE QUALITÉ DU PRODUIT ET LA PERFECTION DE LA FABRICATION
N° 16 CRAMOISI

LANCÔME FRANCE
GARANTIT LA HAUTE QUALITÉ DU PRODUIT ET LA PERFECTION DE LA FABRICATION
N° 23 SOMBRE

24 Av
R.R. 35351 **13**
vernis insolub

LANCÔME FRANCE
IL GARANTIT LA HAUTE QUALITÉ DU PRODUIT ET LA PERFECTION DE LA FABRICATION

BIEN QUE LA PERSONN
CHACUNE DOIVE SE MA
DANS LE CHOIX DU
LANCÔME SUGGÈRE
POUR LE JOUR
AUX BRUNES : LE VERMEIL OU
AUX BLONDES : LE FEU, L'INCARNAT
AUX CHATAINES : LE VERMEIL, L'INCARNAT
AUX ROUSSES : L'ORANGÉ OU L
POUR LE SOIR
L'INCARNAT ET LE CRAMO
MERVEILLE ; QUANT À L
IL RESTE AUSSI PIQUANT A L
ÉLECTRIQUE QU'AU PLEI

22 Mars 1935
R.R. 35291 **13927** Laroche
Mat 2105
E.p. 1150

Conquête LANCÔME FRANCE

TROPIQUES LANCÔME FRANCE

KYPRE LANCÔME FRANCE

TENDRES NUITS LANCÔME FRANCE

BOCAGES LANCÔME FRANCE

24 Avril 1935
R.R. 35330 **13928** Laroche
vernis insoluble Mat 2105
E.p. vernis C
1150

Fête des œillets –
Assistance par le travail
E.p. 1183

6 Juin 1935 **14050** Navarr
Carte teinté
55 ×
E.p. 1184
E.p. 1185

LOTION POUR MISE EN PLIS LANCÔME FRANCE

LOTION À L'EAU DE COLOGNE LANCÔME FRANCE

RÉVOLTE LANCÔME FRANCE
10 Septembre 1936 **15236**

Eau de Cologne CACHET BLEU LANCÔME PARIS FRANCE

Eau de Cologne CACHET BLEU LANCÔME PARIS FRANCE
RR 36518A

Eau de Cologne CACHET BLEU LANCÔME PARIS FRANCE
RR 36518B

23 Août 1938 **17179** Muller
RR 35937 Ingres blanc
47 × 63

5 Décembre 1935 **14483** Prioux
RR 35353 vélin alfa teinté crème
65 × 100 de 28 kos

19 Septemb **15203**
RR 38053

TEN CO TRO BO KYPRE
LA LA LA LA LANCÔME
PARIS PARIS PARIS PARIS FRANCE
RR 35938

FLACON PROVISION CONTENANCE 100 cc

LANCÔME FRANCE
GARANTIT LA HAUTE QUALITÉ DU PRODUIT ET LA PERFECTION DE LA FABRICATION
N° 26 FLAMME

LANCÔME FRANCE
GARANTIT LA HAUTE QUALITÉ DU PRODUIT ET LA PERFECTION DE LA FABRICATION

Laroche 8 Septembre 38
Mat 2105 **17150**
Vernis C RR 42092
eup p. 1150

Gardénia LANCÔME

FLÈCHES LANCÔME

LES CAHIERS

DE

LANCÔME

BEAUTÉ

Voilà...
rubis sur l'ongle

LANCÔME

PARIS   MAQUILLAGE   FRANCE

Jean Droit

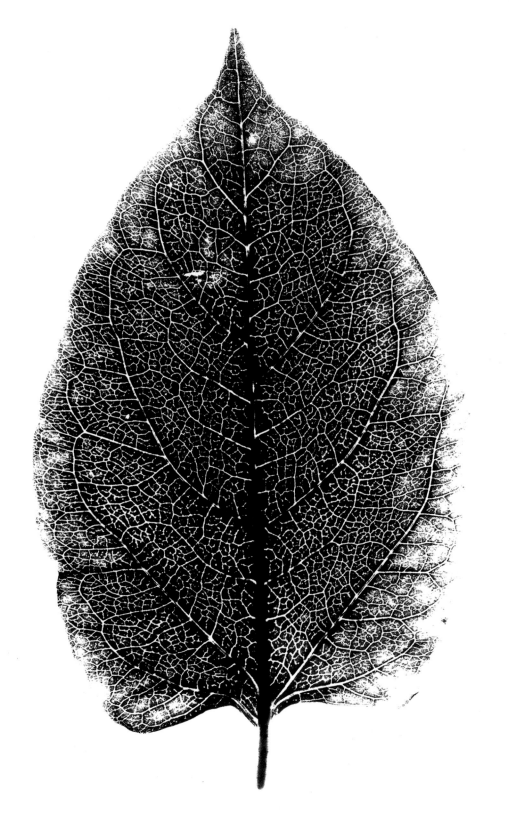

maquillage
d'été
de
LANCÔME

LANCÔME
PARIS

maquillage
d'été
de
LANCÔME

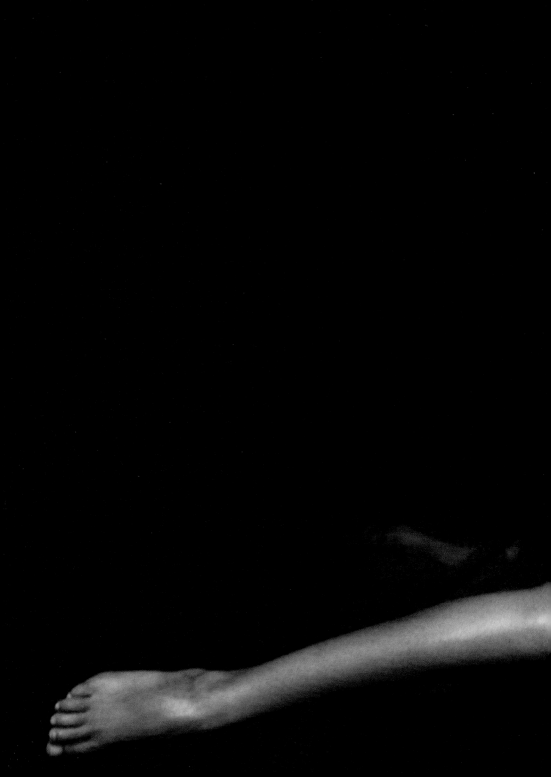

Chronology

Prehistory of Lancôme

Armand Petitjean was born on May 20, 1886, in Saint-Loup-sur-Semouse, in the Haute-Saône department of France. As a young man he went to South America with his brothers, where they ran an import company distributing European goods—everything from champagne to perfume, from fabrics to railway engines.

World War I saw him back in France, where he enlisted. But he was plucked out of the trenches and entrusted with a very special mission—he was asked to bring the countries of South America into the war on the side of the Allies. For part of 1917 he took the ambassadors of Brazil and Chile on a guided tour of France. Petitjean sold them the concept of France as a repository of civilization and taught them to love and appreciate French culture. Brazil and Chile decided to fight to defend France. In short, he succeeded so well that after the war he was offered a post as Ambassador to Brazil, or alternatively, as Minister of Propaganda. Who was the guiding hand behind this glittering ascent? Philippe Berthelot, French Secretary of State for Foreign Affairs.

Armand Petitjean's career was assured. But he knew himself well enough to refuse the glittering offers. While he could achieve the impossible in time of war, he knew he could never achieve such triumphs in peacetime, when France would return as quickly as possible to its comfortable conservatism. Later in life, he was always to use the word "propaganda" in its positive sense, close to the religious sense of "propagation of the faith." He spent his life propagating faith in Lancôme.

1935: February 21, creation of the Lancôme company.
On March 1, the offices and production plant at Courbevoie open their doors.
In June the Institut Lancôme is installed in Paris at 29 rue du Faubourg Saint-Honoré. The first five perfumes are presented to the world at the World Fair in Brussels, together with two eaux de colognes, lipsticks, and *Conquête* face powder.

1942: Creation of the Ecole Lancôme for training women as technical sales staff.

1950: Launch of *Magie*.

1952: Launch of the first *Trésor*. These two fragrances mark Lancôme's arrival as a great international perfume house.

1958: Brussels World Fair. Lancôme, enthroned in the Pavilion of Elegance, wins a gold medal and a diploma *honoris causa*.

1961: Armand-Marcel Petitjean succeeds his father as head of the firm.

1962: On June 20, inauguration of the new production site at Chevilly-Larue, described as the *"Versailles de la Parfumerie."*

June 20, 1962, formal opening of Chevilly-Larue. Armand Petitjean (background) listens to the inaugural speech by his son, Armand-Marcel, who has taken over the reins. © Lancôme Archives.

1964: Lancôme is bought by L'Oréal.

1969: The first Lancôme International Golf Trophy is won by Arnold Palmer.

1970: The production plant is moved from Chevilly to Caudry in northern France. The seventies see the conquest of the American market; the brand wins prime positions in the most important department stores. During the following decade, Lancôme puts down its roots in Asia, always concentrating on the most prestigious outlets.
On September 29, 1970, Armand Petitjean dies at the age of eighty-four.

1983: Isabella Rossellini becomes the face of Lancôme.

1986: A world-beating first, with the launch of *Niosôme*, the anti-age system that was to revolutionize cosmetics. Liposomes (the vectors of the active ingredients) and the principle of biomimetism become the new stars and form the principle areas of research at Lancôme.

1990: Launch of the second *Trésor*, "the perfume of precious moments."

1995: *Poême*, incarnated by Juliette Binoche.

1997: Lancôme makeup becomes more closely associated with fashion with the arrival of makeup magician Fred Farrugia. His seasonal collections, beginning with *Chrysalide* and *Rouge*, attract a great deal of attention.

1996–1998: New faces appear—Cristiana Reali for skin-care and makeup; Inès Sastre for skincare, makeup, and *Trésor*; and Marie Gillain for *Ô oui!*

The cover of Lancômiana, *the house magazine, carried a picture of a rose by the painter Redouté.*
It was this painting that inspired the symbol used for the brand's perfumes. © Lancôme Archives.

LANCÔMIANA

Lancôme d'abord...

Nᵒˢ 29-30

PRINTEMPS ÉTÉ 1956

Lancôme

Marrakech, the first post-war perfume (1947), shown in a double page of the luxurious edition of the Lancôme perfumes catalog, published by Draeger. Bottle designed by Marc Lalique. Box in the national red and green of Morocco. © Photo Laziz Hamani/Éditions Assouline.

The Lancôme shield. The brand was launched in 1935 with a triple emblem: the rose for perfumes, the lotus for skin-care and the cherub for makeup. A bust of Venus signalled the brand's presence in a store. © Lancôme Archives.
Armand Petitjean. When he founded Lancôme he was already fifty years old. He has a nineteenth-century face, but his ideas were far in advance of his time. © Photo Laure Albin Guillot/Family Archives.

This admirably proportioned bottle was intended for a makeup remover, *Lait des Hespérides,* which could also be used as a pre-makeup moisturizer. A lotus flower, symbol of skin-care products, was engraved on the stopper. © Photo Laziz Hamani/ Éditions Assouline.
Isabella Rossellini: from *Portrait d'une femme,* an exhibition of photographs of the actress at the Palais de Tokyo. © Photo Robert Mapplethorpe.

Lancôme had its own jewelery workshops at Cran-Gevrier, near Annecy, where lipstick holders and powder compacts were produced. Here, two lipstick cases: left, *Versailles* in hard lacquer with 14-ct gold cross-hatching; right, *Le Baladin.* © Photo Jacques Boulay.
Image of beauty, lipstick study by a great photographer, which appeared in *Vogue* France in 1958. © Photo Erwin Blumenfeld.

The Institut, at 29 Faubourg Saint-Honoré, is as old as Lancôme itself and has never changed its address. In this display window from the fifties are *Magie, Trésor,* and the *Eaux de Senteur des Quatre Saisons.* © Lancôme Archives.
Inès Sastre in *Rouge,* the 1998–99 Autumn-Winter collection created by Fred Farrugia. The energy of the color and its message of strength have seduced women all over the world. © Photo Javier Vallhonrat/Lancôme.

Blushers existed in two versions. A dry blusher was easy to carry in one's purse for retouches, while the creamy version was larger and stayed on the dressing table. Here, different dry blushers. © Photo Jacques Boulay. **Lancôme's lavender waters** were very well known. During the shortages of the second world war a very concentrated lavender perfume was produced (*La Vallée Bleue,* 1943). Here, an advertisement from 1945 for *Eau de Lavande.* © Lancôme Archives.

Magie has always inspired advertising that has a surreal, fairytale character, like this poster by E. M. Pérot of the Lancôme Studios, reminiscent of Dalí. © Lancôme Archives. **Chrysalide.** A different sort of surrealism can be seen in this beautiful photograph illustrating the metallic reflections of the Spring/Summer 1998 *Chrysalide* collection, created by Lancôme's makeup magician Fred Farrugia. © Photo Torkil Gudnason/Madame Figaro.

Nail varnish. There were some thirty nail varnishes and lacquers, matched to the lipsticks. For the evening, pearlized, silvered, golden, or neon tints were recommended. Advertisement from 1949. © Lancôme Archives.
Clé de Coquette. This brilliantly gilded lipstick holder from 1951 "completely escapes banality thanks to its design and its special slide mechanism, with an automatically closing cover." © Photo Laziz Hamani/Éditions Assouline.

Cachet Bleu is one of the two *Eaux de Cologne* launched in 1935. Despite the name, this was a peach-colored fragrance based on orange flowers. The bottle, nicknamed "the moon-fish" is one of the Lancôme Studio's most beautiful creations. © Photo Jacques Boulay. **Perfume labels,** among which one can recognize *Cachet Bleu* from the holes for the cord with the blue seal. Among the labels is one for a setting lotion, unique in Lancôme's history. © Lancôme Archives.

Les Cahiers de Lancôme. In 1942 Armand Petitjean created the Ecole Lancôme and began publication of the *Cahiers de Lancôme,* using an elegant typography and high-quality paper, "to teach women how to keep themselves beautiful." This issue, devoted to beauty care, was illustrated with statues of Venus and lotus flowers. © Lancôme Archives.

Inès Sastre for *Trésor.* A talented actress as well as a top model, Inès Sastre is of Spanish origin. Despite a crowded schedule she managed to complete her studies in comparative literature at the Sorbonne. The *Trésor* woman also appears in skincare and makeup photographs. © Photo Dominique Isserman/Lancôme.

These narrow bottles with their jasmine-flower stoppers were used to make gift sets of different fragrances in white and gold boxes. It was a successful way of introducing women to the diversity of Lancôme's perfumery. © Photo Laziz Hamani/Éditions Assouline. **Rubis sur l'Ongle,** an advertising campaign from 1946. Rubis was an intensely red nail lacquer. Others were named *Pourpre, Méphisto,* and *Coccinelle.* © Lancôme Archives.

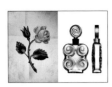

Rose from an illuminated manuscript used by the printer Draeger for the cover of a catalog of Lancôme perfumes. © Photo Laziz Hamani/Éditions Assouline.
Spirals of repolished frosted glass decorate this bottle and its stopper, designed by Jean Sala, with a presentation box by Adrian Leduc. Used for different fragrances. Limited edition, 1944. © Photo Laziz Hamani/Éditions Assouline.

A mysterious leaf, or rather its photograph, found in the Lancôme Archives. Possibly to illustrate the idea of a life-carrying network of veins, or simply the inspiration for another perfume bottle.... © Lancôme Archives. **Juliette Binoche,** photographed by Eiichiro Sakata. She is the muse of *Poême*, launched in 1995. "Say it all without saying a word" is both the advertising caption for the fragrance and Juliette's special gift—she is an Oscar®-winning actress. © Photo E. Sakata/Lancôme.

Lancôme chose this young woman to advertise foundations in 1954–55. The compact foundation *Discoteint* was being promoted for evening use and, curiously enough, for the beach. The window display shows the summer makeup range.

This quiver is obviously meant for the perfume *Flèches*.... Wrong. It held *Magie* and *Trésor*, and was one of the limited editions that Lancôme gave to guests at charity balls. **Trésor I** (1952), in the diamond bottle created by Georges Delhomme. It is the crystal copy of a brilliant-cut diamond. The fragrance "evokes the magnificence of the Orient combined with the taste of Paris." © Photo Laziz Hamani/Éditions Assouline.

In 1952, Lancôme launched a perfume bottle for the purse, shaped like a drop of water. The following year it was renamed "Teardrop" in the USA. It could also be worn on a chain as a pendant. © Photo Keiichi Tahara/Lancôme.

One of the first Lancôme advertisements. A young woman in evening wear shows her friend the standard Lancôme perfume bottle, Georges Delhomme's *Jasmine*. He created it in July 1934. © Lancôme Archives.
Empreinte de Beauté, an astringent beauty mask, was an almost liquid paste whose active ingredients were absorbed by the skin as it dried.

A woman's lipstick case was a jewel in the eyes of Armand Petitjean and should distinguish the woman who used it just as clearly as her rings and her bracelets. This rigorous concept of female elegance was Petitjean's reason for refusing to use disposable holders. Here, eleven fabulously crafted lipstick cases from that elegant era.... © Photo Laziz Hamani/Éditions Assouline.

Trésor **launch.** 1990 saw the launch of *Trésor II,* "the perfume of precious moments." Isabella Rossellini was the star for the new fragrance, and she described *Trésor* as "a perfume with a past, with a memory. You feel when you wear it that you can't be forgotten." © Photo Peter Lindbergh/Lancôme.

Inès Sastre, one of Lancôme's new faces, here *Top Model's* cover story for June 1998. © Photo L. Schmid.

Christmas 1945, perfume gift box by Georges Delhomme: gilded, with five medallions illustrating scenes from the Christian nativity, the rectangular bottle inside had a concealed stopper, providing a continuous surface for a radiant angel worked into the glass. Draeger's catalog. © Photo Laziz Hamani/Éditions Assouline. **The** *Eaux de Senteur. Bel Automne* and *Joyeux Eté* were introduced in 1947, *Grâces du Printemps* in 1952, and *Fêtes de l'hiver* (right page) in 1959. © Photo Jacques Boulay.

Lancôme was never shy of advertising more than one product at a time. Here is the palette offered by the makeup division in 1941: lipstick, dry and cream blushers, and mascara. Not an abundant offering, but it was wartime. © Lancôme Archives. **The mysterious East:** three new lipstick shades, *Bengali, Sari,* and *Mysore* reflect the sixties' taste for oriental exoticism. Photo in *Vogue* France, April 1967. © All rights reserved.

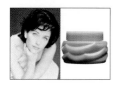

Cristiana Reali, the young Brazilian-Italian actress, whose extraordinary blue eyes promote Lancôme skin-care and makeup. © Photo Claudio Carpi/Lancôme. **The** *Océane* **line.** In the fifties Lancôme launched a complex range of marine-derived care products. Here, a cream presented in a jar sculpted with waves, by Georges Delhomme. © Photo Jacques Boulay.

Ô de Lancôme **bottle** created by Serge Mansau in 1969. This oblong column carved with running water was updated in a frosted version for *Ô oui!* by Gérard Wantz. © Photo Philippe Jacob/Lancôme. **Marie Gillain** was chosen for her youth and her spontaneity. This young actress represents a new generation that is positive and says "Yes" to life and love, and places its optimistic hopes in the third millennium. © Photo André Rau/L'Officiel.

Conquête, one of the first five fragrances that launched Lancôme. Based on a rose concentrate. The bottle gleams with tiny glass pearls, and the stopper catches the light like a crystal ball. Created by Georges Delhomme. © Photo Jacques Boulay. *Gardénia,* or the witchcraft of white flowers.... A star has become embedded in the stopper, and the contents glow with a warm golden light. Bottle by Henri Navarre, 1937. © Photo Jacques Boulay.

The author wishes to thank Armand-Marcel Petitjean for the precious documents which he kindly leant her, and his daughter Clara for giving access to the family archives.

The publisher wishes to thank the House of Lancôme for their help in the preparation of this book.

The publisher also acknowledges Juliette Binoche, Marie Gillain, Cristiana Reali, Isabella Rossellini and Inès Sastre, as well as Jacques Boulay, Harry Brejat, Claudio Carpi, Fred Farrugia, Torkil Gudnason, Laziz Hamani, Dominique Issermann, Philippe Jacob, Peter Lindbergh, André Rau, Eiichiro Sakata, Lothar Schmid, Keiichi Tahara and Javier Vallhonrat.

Finally, this book would not have been possible without the kind contributions of David Abel (*Vogue* US/Editions Condé Nast), Josette Arrigoni (Artmedia), Kathleen Blumenfeld, Angela Carbonetti (William Morris Agency), Anne Hermeline (V.M.A.), Vanessa Jérôme, Patricia Lejeune (City), Emmanuelle Montet (Musée de la Mode et du Costume), Odile (Olivier Rozet), Publicis, Sandrine et Hélène (Filomeno), Rosanna Sguera (Art + Commerce), Sylvie Soulier-Biais (*Madame Figaro*) and Jean Tissier (*L'Officiel*).